Sylheti Proverbs & Idioms

A collection of very amusing Sylheti Proverbs & Idioms transliterated and translated to English.

Shumi.

If you purchase this book without a cover, or a PDF, jpg, or tiff copy of this book, it is likely a stolen property or a counterfeit. In that case neither the author(s), the publisher, nor any of the employees or agents has received any payment for the copy. We urge you to please not purchase any such copy.

Illustrations in this book have been drawn and edited by the Author.

Copyright © 2020 Shumi

All rights reserved.

ISBN: 9798577917753

ACKNOWLEDGEMENTS

This small book is dedicated to the Sylheti parents that uprooted to seek a better future for themselves and their children.

Thank you to my parents and knowledgeable acquaintances that I have been fortunate to have in my life, who have continued their Bengali traditions and given me a taste of Sylheti life.

Introduction

Like many of you, I am a British Bangladeshi. I was born and raised in the UK. Both of my parents emigrated from Bangladesh many years ago. They left their humble beginnings, their cattle and the torrential weather at a very young age to earn a better living here in the UK and to provide a better future for the generations to come.

I wouldn't say that I am extremely fluent in Bengali speaking and writing, but let's just say I do speak Sylheti well enough (with a slight London twang) to get by and hold a conversation. Sylheti is the Indic language spoken in the North-eastern region of Bangladesh. It is a colloquial dialect of Bengali/Bangla.

So, I speak Sylheti with my parents and elders. With the rest of the world I speak English, including my siblings, relatives, friends, neighbours, colleagues... you get the jist. If you're like me, then you probably speak, read & write more English than you do Bengali/Sylheti and you may be yearning to reconnect with the traditional Sylheti lingo.

I've written this book today as a token to the British Sylheti community of my era. I don't know about you, but growing up in a western society meant that we didn't always experience first-hand the values, the traditions and cultural aspects of the Sylheti lands as much as we may have wanted to. Learning and studying in English just so happens to take over our lives, as we aim to become successful in the English speaking world to earn a living and integrate with our British communities. As I have grown older (and now wiser - I hope), I have come to admire and appreciate the beauty of our Sylheti and Bengali traditions, music, the language and VERY amusing Pro-verbs & Idioms!

There were always certain phrases I would come across; whether it be from eaves dropping on conversations between Uncles in the living room about their frustrations on the Awami League, or from yelling over a long- distance 7p a minute phone call to relatives or from the variety of authentic Bengali Sky Channels!

Some of these pro-verbs/idioms are quite aggressive, some are funny, some are bitter sweet, some are motivational and some are just harsh truths. On most occasions, I didn't understand what on earth they were referring to, given a lot of Bengali/Sylheti sayings are heavily metaphorical and require 'reading between the lines' to understand it's true meaning and why it was used in a certain situation.

Anyhow, I have collected the transliterations of a handful of Sylheti Proverbs in this book (of which some of them originate from proper 'Shudoh' Bangla) and translated them to English (with the help of some family members and friends) - and a good laugh it was too trying to decipher these!

Some of the Sylheti proverbs when translated to English do sound absolutely hilarious... so, I warn you now, you'll either love it or hate!

I hope you enjoy these Proverbs & Idioms as much as I did, and I hope you too will have a chuckle or two with the rest of your families and friends.

Shumi.

In this book you will find 65 proverbs and Idioms written in the following format:

English Transliteration
In the colloquial Sylheti form i.e. how a Sylheti speaking person would actually say and pronounce it verbally.

Bengali Sanskrit text
The written text of the proverb, if it were to be read in the 'proper' (shudoh) form of Bangla.

English Translation
The proverb/idiom written in English form.

The meaning of the proverb/idiom
A description in English of what is meant by the phrase.

Illustration
A rough drawing sketched by the author to mimic the Proverb/Idiom ☺

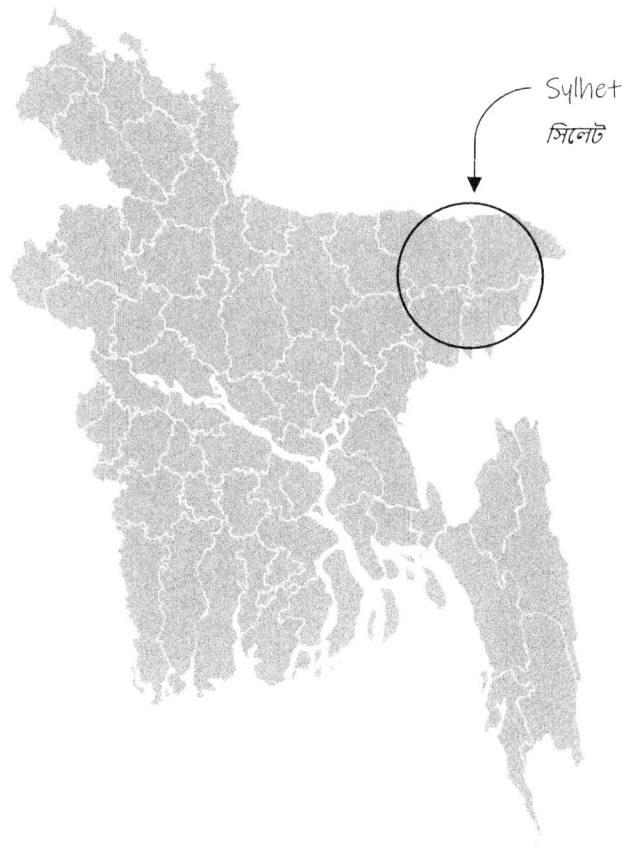

Brace yourself...

1

Nay Mamu Thaki Khana Mamu Bala
(নাই মামার চেয়ে কানা মামা ভাল।)

***

"A blind uncle is better than no uncle."

***

This proverb tells us to appreciate what you have. Having something is better than nothing.

'Mamu' is maternal uncle - it is used in this proverb because the bond with an uncle is usually considered to be warm and loving.

2

Nasteh Na Janleh Ootan Therah

(নাচতে না জানলে উটান তেরা।)

***

"Can't dance, because the ground is wonky."

———

***

This proverb is used as a figure of speech, often mentioned when someone is blaming something/someone else for not being able to do or complete a task.

3

Chok Chok Khorleh, Shuna Oy Na

(চকচক করলেই সোনা হয় না।)

***

"Sparkle and shine, doesn't mean it's always gold."

———

***

This proverb is used to state that "all that glitters is not gold", so don't be deceived by what you see, or don't always trust an appearance.

4

Thelor Mathat, Thel Dewah

(তৈলাক্ত মাথা তেল দেওয়াহ।)

***

"Oiling one's head that is already oiled."

***

This proverb is used when someone is trying to advise or help one that needs no help, instead of helping the one that IS in need.

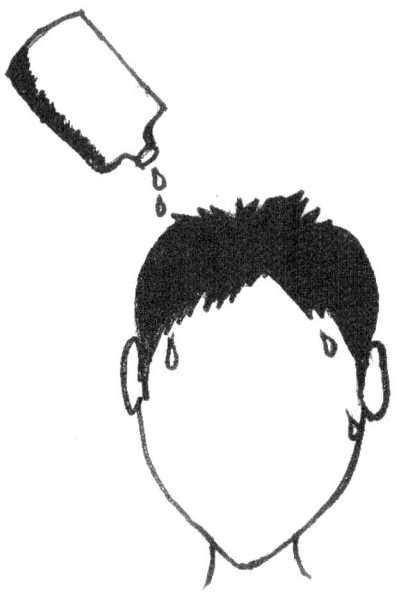

5

Cheshta Sara Kicchu Oy Na

(চেষ্টা না করে কিছুই হয় না।)

***

"Without trying, nothing can be done."

———

***

This is a motivational proverb advising that one should at least try before giving up. If you don't try you will never know.

6

Doosh Khalyeh, Hoosh Oy

(ডুশ খাইলে হুশ হয়।)

***

"A bump will make you alert."

———

***

This is used when you've had a bump or been knocked in life. To lighten up the situation this is said to portray that you are now more alert. The proverb is usually said both when someone has been knocked physically or has experienced an unfortunate event.

'A few knocks in life will make you stronger.'

7

Shida Anguleh Ghee Ooteh Na

(সিদা আঙুল ঘি তুলতে পারে না।)

***

"Ghee cannot be scooped out with a straight finger."

———

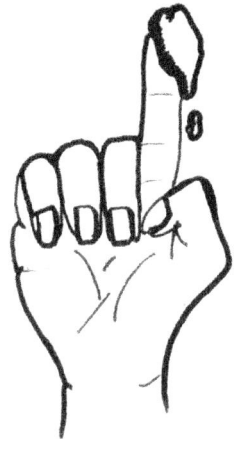

***

This proverb is used when you've requested something of someone in a polite manner, however they do not listen or oblige, hence it forces you to be stern/harsh when making a request or asking them for something.

If you were to attempt to scoop out Ghee (clarified hard butter) with a straight finger and pull it straight back out, no ghee can be lifted out. But if you curve or crook your finger then you will successfully scoop out some of that ghee.

8

Ageh Geleh Baageh Khai, Khoreh Geleh Foisha Fyn

(প্রথম হন তবে বাঘ খাবে, শেষ পর্যন্ত যান তবে টাকা পাবেন।)

***

"If you're first the tiger will eat you, if you go last the money will find you."

***

Usually when someone tries to innovate or pioneer an idea for the first time, they may not succeed at first. They often might fail or their idea may not be the best. Eventually the idea can be improved by someone else to enhance and make profit.

Basically.... "First the worst, second the best!"

9

Goorar Dim!
(ঘোড়ার ডিম।)

***

"Horses egg!"

———

***

An impossible thing - As horses don't actually lay eggs! This idiom is said when you believe something to be bullshit.

10

Ekh Ateh Tali Bazeh Na

(এক হাতে তালি বাজে না।)

***

"You can't clap with one hand."

———

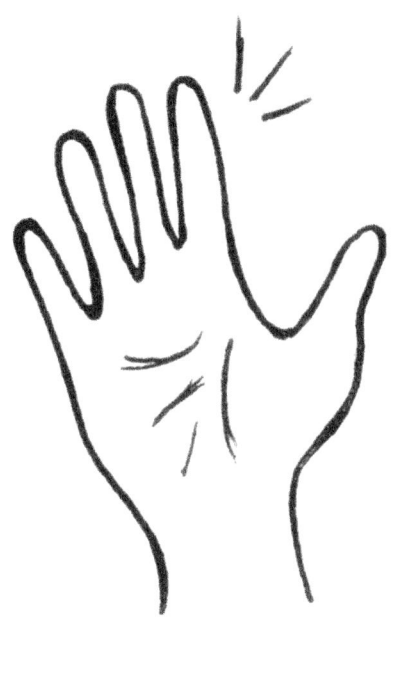

***

This proverb is highlighting that it "takes two to tango" or that there are two sides to every story. Or that it takes two to quarrel!

11

Ekh Tileh Dui Pakhi Mara
(এক ঢিলে দুই পাখি মারা।)

***

"Hit two birds with one stone."

———

***

This is a positive proverb. It is used when one
hopes to complete, achieve, or take care
of two tasks or problems at the same time or with a
singular series of actions.

12

Dakka Na Khayleh, Fakka Oytay Nay

(ডাক্কা না খাইলে, পাকা হবে না।)

***

"Got knocked and became like concrete."

Or "If you didn't get a few knocks you won't become like concrete."

***

A few knocks/bumps/crashes in life will make you stronger. This proverb is often mentioned both in metaphorical and physical situations.

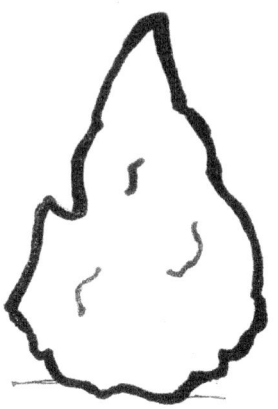

13

Gadah Reh Fitleh Goorah Oyna
(গাধা পিটে ঘোড়া হয় না।)

***

"If you whip a donkey it doesn't turn into a horse."

———

***

Persistently trying to change an inadequate person won't work. This proverb is used when you are asking something of someone that continues to let you down.

14

Khewr Poush Mash, Khewr Shobanash

(কারও পৌষ মাষ কারও সর্বনাশ।)

***

"One person's harvest months, is another person's complete devastation."

———

***

This proverb is used when something, someone, an event or some place is good for one person but may not be good for another.

15

Khazna Thaki, Bazna Beshi

(খাজনা থাকি ভজনা বেশি।)

***

"Its noise is louder than its worth."

———

***

Khazna refers to wealth/value. Bazna is referred to as noise. This proverb is used when someone is exaggerating the value of an item or substance or boasting his/her wealth.

Or when the face value of an item that a person intends to purchase is overestimated and hyped, exceeding its actual value.

16

Kilor Khatol Kill Na Khayleh Fakheh Na

(কিলের কাঁঠাল কিল না খাইলে পাক্কে না।)

***

"A Jackfruit without a few beats won't ripen."

***

Beat it to make it sweet. There is a particular jackfruit in South Asia that is said to become sweeter if given a few thumps. This proverb is used metaphorically when one is trying to portray that someone 'needs to be put in their place'. – Not physically of course, this might be through a few stern words.

17

Kilor Khatol Killeh Fakheh, Na Khayle Soi Mash Takheh

(কিলর কাঁঠল কিলে পাক্কে, না খাইলে ছয় মাস থাকে।)

***

"A Jackfruit needs a few thumps to ripen. And if it doesn't get thumped it will be left alone for 6 months."

***

This proverb is used metaphorically when someone 'needs to be put in their place' and if they are not put in their place, they are left alone, disliked by the majority; i.e. left to rot.

18

Baro Masheh Thero Phool Futeh

(বারো মাসে তের ফুল।)

***

"In 12 months 13 flowers grow."

———

***

An abundance of festivals. This idiom is used when there are so many events happening and is used to describe the numerous events.

19

Khata Diya, Khata Thoola

(কাঁটা দিয়ে কাঁটা তোলা।)

***

"Pick a thorn with a thorn."

***

Solve a problem with another problem; or one thorn drives away another thorn.

This is similar to the saying "Set a thief to catch a thief".

This proverb is used in situations to get back at a person using the same techniques/characteristic he/she may have used to be malicious/spiteful.

20

Gaaseh Dal Dhilayleh, Gaas Ar Khatazay Na

(গাছে ডাল দিলে, গাছ আর কাটা যায় না।)

***

"When the tree has branched out, it's difficult to cut its roots."

***

This proverb is used in some situations when it's difficult to cut ties completely with something or someone. For example when you have formed a relationship with someone or you have collectively done something together e.g. had children.

21

Nizor Goro Shob Raja

(নিজর ঘরে সব রাজা।)

***

"Everyone is a king in their own home."

***

Every man's home is his castle and so he may sometimes feel the right to treat people as he wishes- which may not always be nice! This proverb may be said out of spite.

22

Bandor Reh Gass Bawa Hikka Yo Na

(বান্দের রে গাছ বাওয়া শিক্ষায়ো না।)

***

"Don't teach a monkey to climb trees."

***

A monkey already knows how to climb trees, hence this proverb is usually said when someone is attempting to tell or teach something that one already knows.

23

Bandor Reh Maya Khorleh Mathath Ootizay

(বান্দার রে মায়া খোরলেহ মাথাই ওটিজায় ।)

***

"Show love to a monkey and it will sit on your head."

———

***

When you show love or sometimes help the wrong person they will or may take advantage of you. Obviously 'sitting on someone's head' is not nice and implies disrespect.

24

Soyteh Mora
(সোয়েতেহ মরা।)

***

"Touch it, it dies."

———

***

This idiom is used sarcastically when someone exaggerates pain or heartbreak.

For example some toddlers may cry their heads off when you attempt to play with their toy.

25

Ekh Bar Na Farleh, Dekho Shotho Bar
(এক বার না ফারলে, দেখো শত বার।)

***

"If you can't do it once, try 100 times."

———

***

We hear this proverb often when struggling to succeed at something. It basically tells us that if at first you don't succeed just keep on trying.

26

Khoro, Nay Moro

(কর অথবা মর।)

***

"Do or Die."

———

***

Do it, or don't do it – either way the person that says this just simply doesn't care.

This idiom is sometimes said in frustration, when you can't be bothered to respond to a person's question.

27

Nizor Doosh, Khew Dekhe Na

(নিজের দুশ কেউ দেখে না।)

***

"Nobody sees their own faults."

***

Quite obviously, one doesn't see their own flaws and shortcomings and so this is often said when trying to reason with or make transparent someone's faults.

28

Sinta Bhabna Khorio Kham

(ভাবিয়া করিও কাজ।)

***

"Think before acting on your work."

———

***

This proverb pretty much says it as it is. In other words, think before you act or look before you leap.

29

Goro Nai Bath, Bandiye Aggeh Thero Zath

(ঘোরেঃ নাই ভাত, বান্দিয়ে আগে তেরো জাত।)

***

"No rice at home, but she shits 13 different types of shit."

***

This proverb is used when someone is showing off. It implies that one is struggling with the bare necessities of feeding oneself yet still produces different types of shit.

30

Amar Kholja

(আমার কলজা !)

***

"My Liver!"

***

This idiom is sometimes said by a person in frustration when responding to another person who may be asking too many questions about what to eat.

31

Amar Matha

(আমার মাথা!)

***

"My Head!"

***

This Idiom is sometimes said in frustration in response to too many questions about what to do or when constantly asking someone about what something is.

32

Khaya Moro

(খাইয়া মর!)

***

"Eat and Perish!"

***

This idiom is said humorously or sarcastically in response to someone who may be over-indulging.

33

Khayleh Fostay Bay, Na Khayleh Fostay Bay

(খাইলে ফস্টাইবাঃ, না খাইলে ফস্টাইবাঃ।)

***

"If you eat it you'll regret it, if you don't eat it you'll regret it."

***

When someone is indecisive about whether they should do something, or usually eat something, this proverb is used when expressing a dilemma.

34

Latti Zar, Matthi Thar
(লাটি যার মাটি তার।)

★★★

"Whoever owns the baton, owns the land."

***

Back in the day when people fought for land, whoever was the stronger party i.e. owned good weapons or had good fighters, that party would ultimately conquer the land. Similarly this proverb is used as a figure of speech representing an individual or an institution's precedence, perhaps because they have power or money which allows them to obtain something just as they wanted it.

35

Phooler Forisoy

(ফুল দ্বারা পরিচিত।)

***

"Known by the flower."

***

A person can be known by the fruits of their labour,
or they may be known because of their offspring.
This can be said both in a good and bad context.

36

Ekh Zoner Mangsho, Onyo Zoner Beesh

(এক ব্যক্তির মাংস অন্য ব্যক্তির বিষ।)

***

"One person's meat is another person's poison."

***

This proverb describes that what's meant for someone else, isn't meant for you. Don't delve into other people's lives or show traits of jealousy. What is good for some people, most often is bad for others.

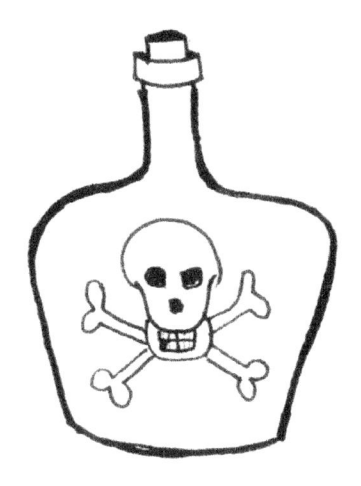

37

Golar Niseh Gelleh, Ar Monoh Takheh Na

(গলার নীচে গেলে, আর মনে রাখবেন না।)

***

"Once it's gone below the throat, you no longer remember it."

***

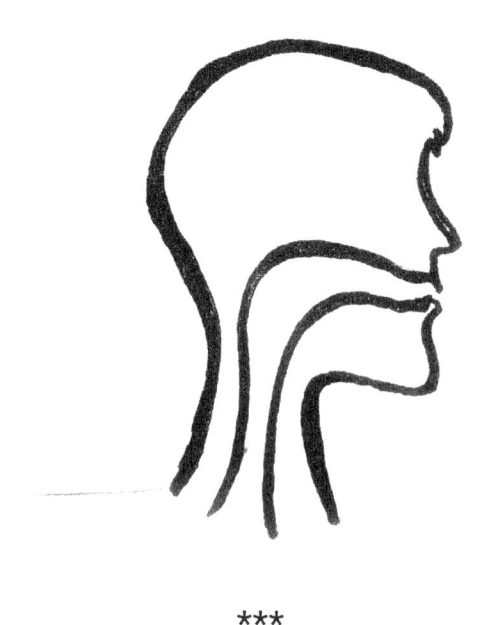

Usually when you eat something you eventually forget what you ate. Similarly once something has been said by someone that is not valued by another, it is forgotten. This proverb somewhat describes cancel culture.

38

Sasa Re Sasa, Amar Zaan Basa

(চাচা আপন জান বাঁচা।)

***

"Oh dear uncle save my life."

***

Everyone for himself or everyone looks after his own. This is used scornfully and is mentioned when one has observed selfish attributes in someone.

We often might hear one say in English - 'Every man for himself'.

39

Ekh Mukeh Dui Khotah

(এক মুখ দুটি কথা বলে।)

***

"One mouth speaks two words."

***

When someone is contradicting themselves or saying two opposing things. This proverb is used when calling out hypocrisy or perhaps 'two faced' people.

40

Koroj Nai, Khoshto Nai

(কর্জ নাই, কষ্টও নাই।)

***

"No debt, no hardship."

———

***

'Out of debt, out danger.' This proverb is illustrating that as long as you don't have loans and debts then surely you have no trouble and are living life.

41

Khawar Mangsho, Khawai Khay Na

(কাকের মাংস কাকে খায় না।)

***

"One Raven will not eat another Raven's meat."

***

Ravens are known to be carnivorous, violent, vigorous animals yet it won't hurt another Raven. This proverb is used when like-minded individuals that you may not necessarily agree with, stick up for one another.

42

Khata Gar Mazeh Nunor Sita Mara

(কাটা গায়ে নুনের ছিটা দেওয়া।)

***

"To sprinkle salt into the wound."

***

This metaphorical Proverb is used when someone may be making an already difficult situation worse. Obviously sprinkling salt into a wound would sting!

43

Khaan Tanleh, Mathah Ayboh

(কান টানলে মাথা আসে।)

***

"If you pull the ear, the head will follow."

———

***

Given one, the other will follow. This proverb might be used when an individual is following the crowd and not thinking of the consequences of an action for himself. A person who always agrees/supports an opinion of their peer/superior.

44

Ekh Fooleh Mala Oy Na

(একটি ফুল একটি মালা তৈরি করে না।)

***

"One flower doesn't make a garland."

***

This proverb is used to encourage one to work as a team. You may not be able to accomplish a task by yourself, it is better to work together.

45

Koyla Doyleh, Moylah Zay Na

(কয়লা ধুলে ময়লা যায় না।)

***

"Washing charcoal, won't clean the dirt."

***

This proverb is used when describing that one's nature remains unchanged, no matter how hard you try to advise them for something better or good.

When you attempt to clean charcoal it will still look dirty because that is the nature of coal.

46

Khata Sara Phool Oy Na

(কাটা ছারা ফুল হয় না।)

***

"Without a thorn there is no rose."

***

This proverb is portraying that without pain there is no gain. In order for a rose to blossom it must grow its thorns. Likewise if you strive and plough through the difficulties in life you will indeed succeed.

47

Tekhia Hikka

(ভুল করুন এবং শিখুন।)

***

"Make mistakes and learn."

***

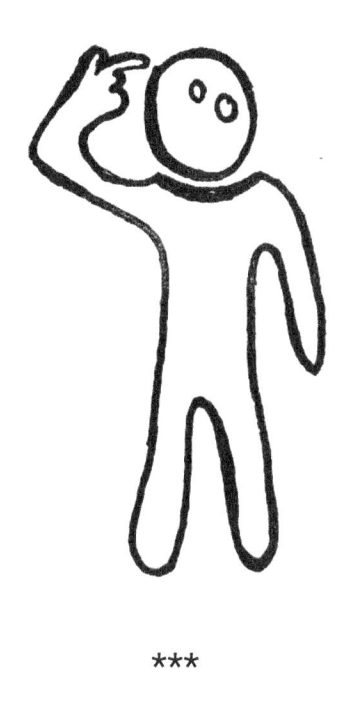

This proverb is usually said when someone has made a mistake and landed in a difficult situation. It's often in these situations that you will 'learn from your mistakes.'

48

Thara Thari Khorleh Zinish Kharaf Oy

(তাড়াতাড়ি করলে কাজ ভাল হয় না।)

***

"If you rush, then your task will be ruin."

***

This proverb is highlighting that rushing any piece of work may ruin the quality of it.

Essentially "haste makes waste."

49

Dosh Zoneh Milya Khoro Kham

(দশে মিলে করি কাজ।)

***

"Work together in a team of ten."

———

***

When you need to get a job done or need to resolve a problem this proverb is used to advise that two or more heads are better than one, or the more the merrier. Delegate and be efficient.

50

Daat Thakhteh Mulyo Booza Zai Na

(দাঁত থাকতে দাঁতের মর্যাদা বোঝা যায় না।)

***

"You don't realise the value of teeth while you still have them."

***

This proverb is used when you don't realise the worth of something until it is gone, or you don't realise what you have until it is gone.

We often take teeth for granted until they start dropping out one by one.

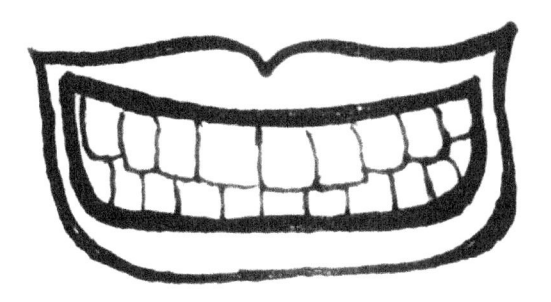

51

Beshi Mithai Fet Khateh
(বেশি মিষ্টি পেট কাটে।)

***

"Too much sweet, gives you stomach cramps."

***

This proverb might be said when anticipating that a good thing might come to an end. Usually we say that 'too much of anything is no good.'

52

Itcha Thakleh, Oofay Hoy

(ইচ্ছা থাকিলেই উপায় হয়।)

***

"If you have the intention, you can make it happen".

***

This proverb states that if you have the intention to do something then surely you will be successfully in making it happen – "Where there's a will, there is a way."

53

Baffor Beta, Gasor Goota

(বাপের বেটা, গাছর গুটা।)
***

"Like father like son, like bud like tree."

***

This proverb can be used both negatively and positively. It is usually said when someone resembles their father in some way, either in terms of appearance or because of their behavior.

54

Othi Salakher Golai Dori

(অতি চালাকের গলায় দড়ি।)

***

"Too much scheming/cunningness will choke you."

***

When you have achieved something by being deceitful and sly, it will often reveal itself. This proverb in other words means: "Too much cunningness will come back for you."

55

Khoshto Na Khorleh, Fol Mileh Na

(কষ্ট ছাড়া কেষ্ট মেলে না।)

***

"Without hard work you will see no reward."

***

This motivational proverb is used to highlight that hard work is a concept that must be valued. If you work hard at something you will most definitely gain the reward of the work you put in.

56

Jemon Kormo, Themon Fol

(যেমন কর্ম তেমন ফল।)

***

"You get what you give".

***

This proverb is similar to the saying "You sow what you reap". Eventually in life you may have to face up to the consequences of your actions whether it be good or bad.

57

Ajker Raja, Khalker Fokir

(আজ বাদশা কাল ফকির।)

***

"A king today is a beggar tomorrow."

***

This proverb is highlighting that what you have been blessed with today, you may not be blessed with tomorrow.

So it would be wise to always show gratitude for what you do have.

58

Bala Oyteh, Foysha Lageh Na

(ভাল থাকার জন্য টাকা লাগে না।)

***

"Being respectful doesn't cost you money."

***

This proverb is telling us that "Courtesy costs nothing". Simply being courteous is appreciated by everyone and usually does go a long way.

59

Shesh Bala Zaarr, Shob Bala Thaar

(শেষ ভাল যার, সব ভাল তার।)

***

"If his end is well, his beginning is well."

***

If the outcome of a situation is good/pleasant, this compensates for any previous difficulty or unpleasantness that you may have had over a period of time. This is similar to the saying: 'All's well that ends well'.

60

Jotho Ashi, Otho Khanda

(যত হাসি তত কান্না।)

***

"Much laughter, much cry."

***

This proverb is used to portray that if you laugh today you will equally cry tomorrow. Life is not always rainbows and sunshine.

61

Soor Gelehgee, Budhi Bareh

(চোর পালালে বুদ্ধি বাড়ে।)

***

"After the thief leaves, the brain works."

***

This proverb is used when you realise what you should have or could have done once an unnerving event has already happened. We tend to replay events in our minds once it's already happened and then think of things that could have been done better in hind sight.

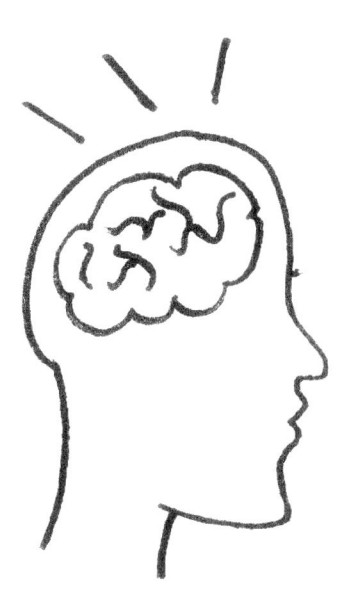

62

Obahbeh Shobab Noshto

(অভাবে স্বভাব নষ্ট।)

***

"Lack of means, causes corruption."

***

This proverb means that being desperate and having no means may lead you to become corrupted or do things that are not necessarily legal. This is similar to the saying:
'Necessity knows no laws'.

63

Ekh Maghe Sheeth Zay Na

(এক মাঘে শীত যায় না।)

***

"One month of rain, won't make the cold go away."

***

Magh is the name of a month in Bengali. In this month it often rains. This proverb is said to mean that, although a sign of something good has happened once, the situation may not continue to be good, and you cannot rely on it.

In English this is similar to the saying: 'One swallow doesn't make a summer'. Swallow is a bird and here it refers to the arrival of the birds at the beginning of summer.

64

Zur Zaar, Moolook Thar

(জোর যার মুল্লুক তার।)

***

"Power/might has the right."

***

This proverb is used to say that people who have power are able to do what they want because no one can stop them. It's often said when someone is being stubborn.

65

Saboreh Newah Foleh

(সাবর এটি পুরস্কার আছে।)

***

"Patience has its rewards."

***

We often say that 'Patience (sabr) is a virtue'. One of the reasons that patience is a virtue is that it involves going through suffering at times, without getting saddened. It involves trusting God that things will happen not in your time, but in God's time.

The ability to wait for something without getting angry or upset is a valuable quality in a person. We sometimes hear the phrase:

'Patience is bitter but its fruit is sweet.'

Shesh!

শেষ !

The End!

More often than not, we come across a lot of sayings and phrases in many languages. Of which, most of them are pieces of advice or just food for thought.

In this book I have collected the transliterations of a bunch of Sylheti Proverbs & Idioms and translated them to English (with the help of some family members and friends) - and a good laugh it was too trying to decipher these!

Some of these pro-verbs/idioms are quite aggressive, some are quite funny, some are bitter sweet, some are motivational and some are just harsh truths. On most occasions, I didn't understand what on earth they were referring to, given a lot of Bengali/Sylheti sayings are heavily metaphorical and require 'reading between the lines' to understand it's true meaning and why it was said in a certain situation.

Some Sylheti proverbs when translated to English do sound absolutely hilarious, so I warn you now, you'll either laugh or cry!

So grab your saa (tea) or tie your longhi and have a good read...

Shumi.

ISBN: 9798577917753

Printed in Great Britain
by Amazon